The Brandywine Watershed

This book belongs to:

_____

*A portion of the sale of this book
supports water stewardship and education*

Can He Keep It?

Written by: Connie Nye
Illustrated by: Anne Wertheim

CAN HE KEEP IT?

Copyright © 2020 by Constance Nye

All rights reserved.
No part of this publication may be reproduced, distributed, or transmitted in any form or by any means –
electronic or mechanical, including photocopy, recording, or any information storage and retrieval system
now known or to be invented – without the prior written permission from the author,
except in the case of brief quotations embodied in critical reviews
and certain noncommercial uses permitted by copyright law.

ISBN: 978-1-7923-2985-2 (hardback)

First Edition   10   9   8   7   6   5   4   3   2   1

Library of Congress Control Number: 2020900973

Printed in the United States by Jostens in Clarksville, Tennessee

Illustrations by Anne Wertheim; rendered in Adobe® Photoshop®

Designed by Elsa Kauffman; text type: Adventuring and Montserrat

For more information, visit www.sweetwatered.com

Summary: Tyson catches a tadpole that he wants to keep. Should he?

Dedicated to all the kids throughout the years
that asked the question,
"Can I keep it?"
And to my Mom and Dad, Bette and Jack,
who made so many things possible.

Special thanks to Eliza for turning
this scenario into the first draft of this book
and to Sydney and Eliza
for always being by my side.

4

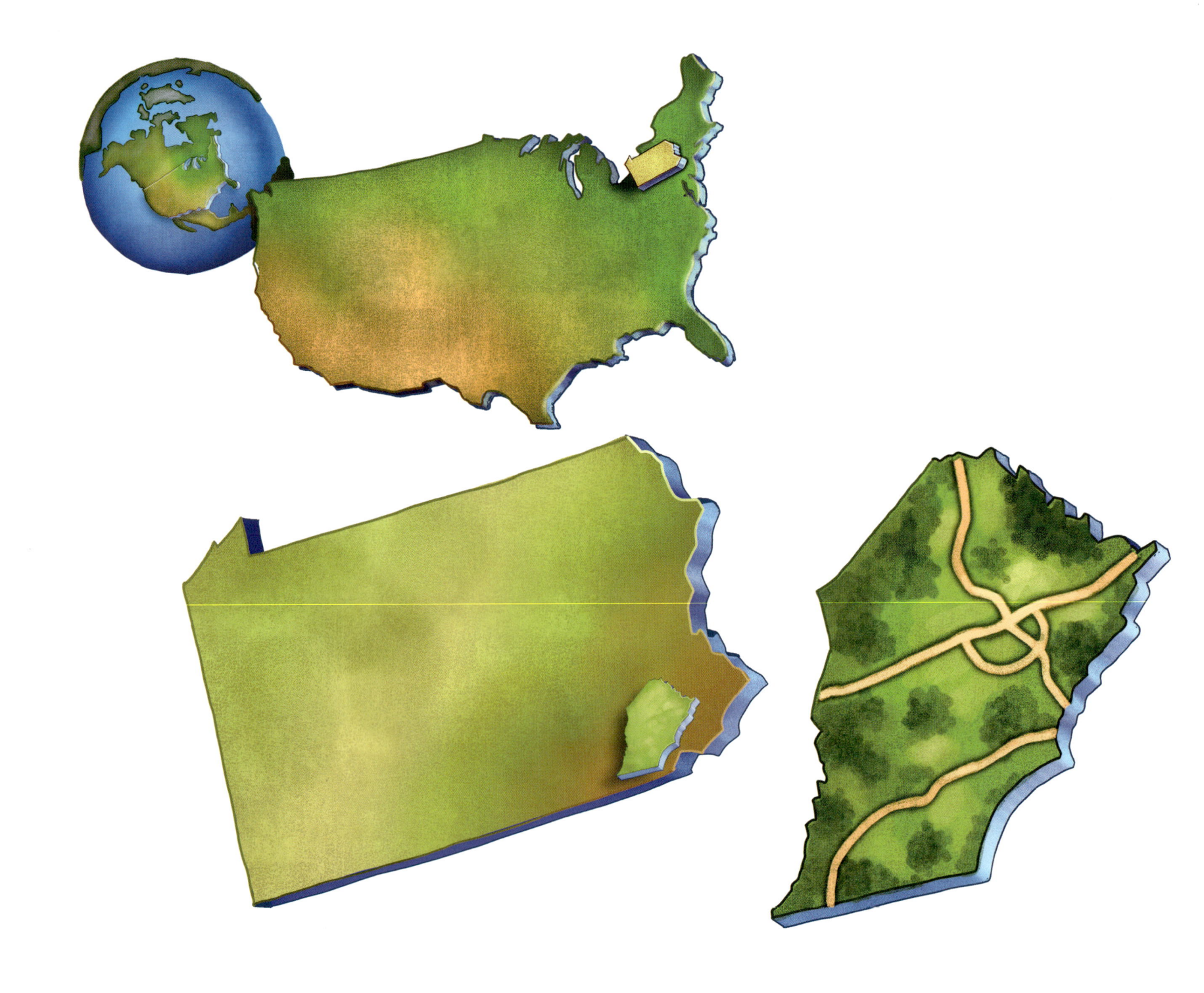

In his own town,

on his own street,

in his own home,

in his own room,

in his own bed,

Tyson slept soundly.

In the middle of his morning stretch, Tyson remembered what today was.

yawwwnnnnn

"Don't forget your boots for pond day," said his mother cheerfully while Tyson ate his breakfast.

On the way to school, Tyson imagined catching something **exciting** at the pond.

When Ms. Nye the science gal arrived, she lined the students up at the front of the classroom. Then, quiet as coyotes, they walked down the hallway and headed outdoors.

At the pond, Ms. Nye divided the students into teams for critter catching.

Then she went over the rules.

Stay with your team!

First thing, get water in your cups!

Be gentle with the critters!

Be sure to share!

Take turns with the equipment!

13

"Whoa!" called Tyson as he watched something *wriggle* out of the mud in his net.

He lifted the tadpole gently, examined it closely, and placed it into his team's cup of water.

Tyson raced over to Ms. Nye with the cup in his hand.

"*Look, look, Ms. Nye, a tadpole! I named it **Taddy**!*"

Can I keep it?

Ms. Nye looked at the tadpole and then at Tyson.
"**Taddy's** a beauty all right," she said.
"And I understand that you would want
to keep him. But think for a minute.

What if a
grEAT BIG GIAnt
was on a field trip
with his class?

And the
GREAT BIG GIANT
scooped you up,
and he said, **'Whoa'**
as he watched
you *wriggle* around
in his net.

Then he lifted you up gently and examined you closely.

And then the **GREAT BIG GIANT** raced over to his teacher and said,

*'Look, look, Mr. Giant Teacher, a kid. I named it **Kiddo**!'*

Can I keep it?

What would you want the **grEAT BIG GIAnt** *to do?"* asked Ms. Nye. "Keep you? Or put you back?"

hmmmmm

Tyson thought for a few moments.

25

26

27

28

"So," said Ms. Nye to Tyson, "*what do you think you should do?*"

That same night...

in his own town,

on his own street,

in his own home,

in his own room,

in his own bed,

Tyson slept soundly.

And so did...

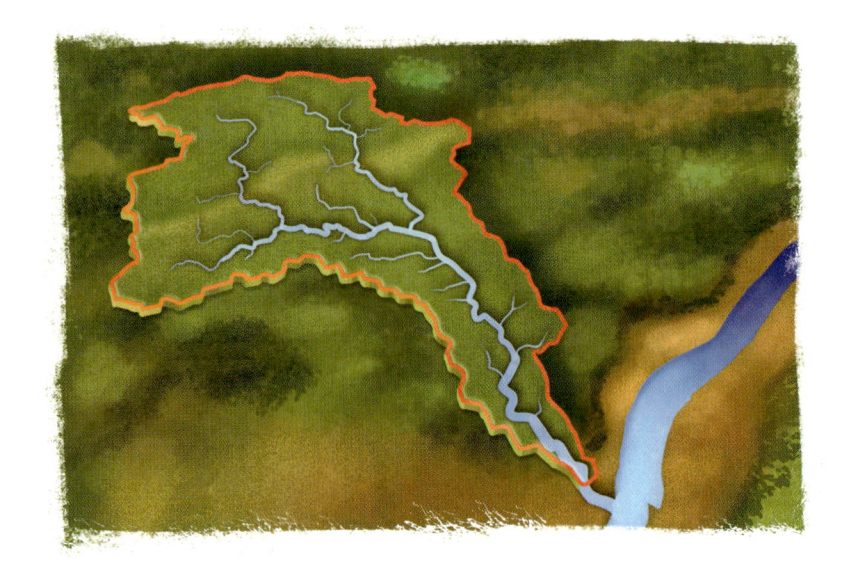

32

33

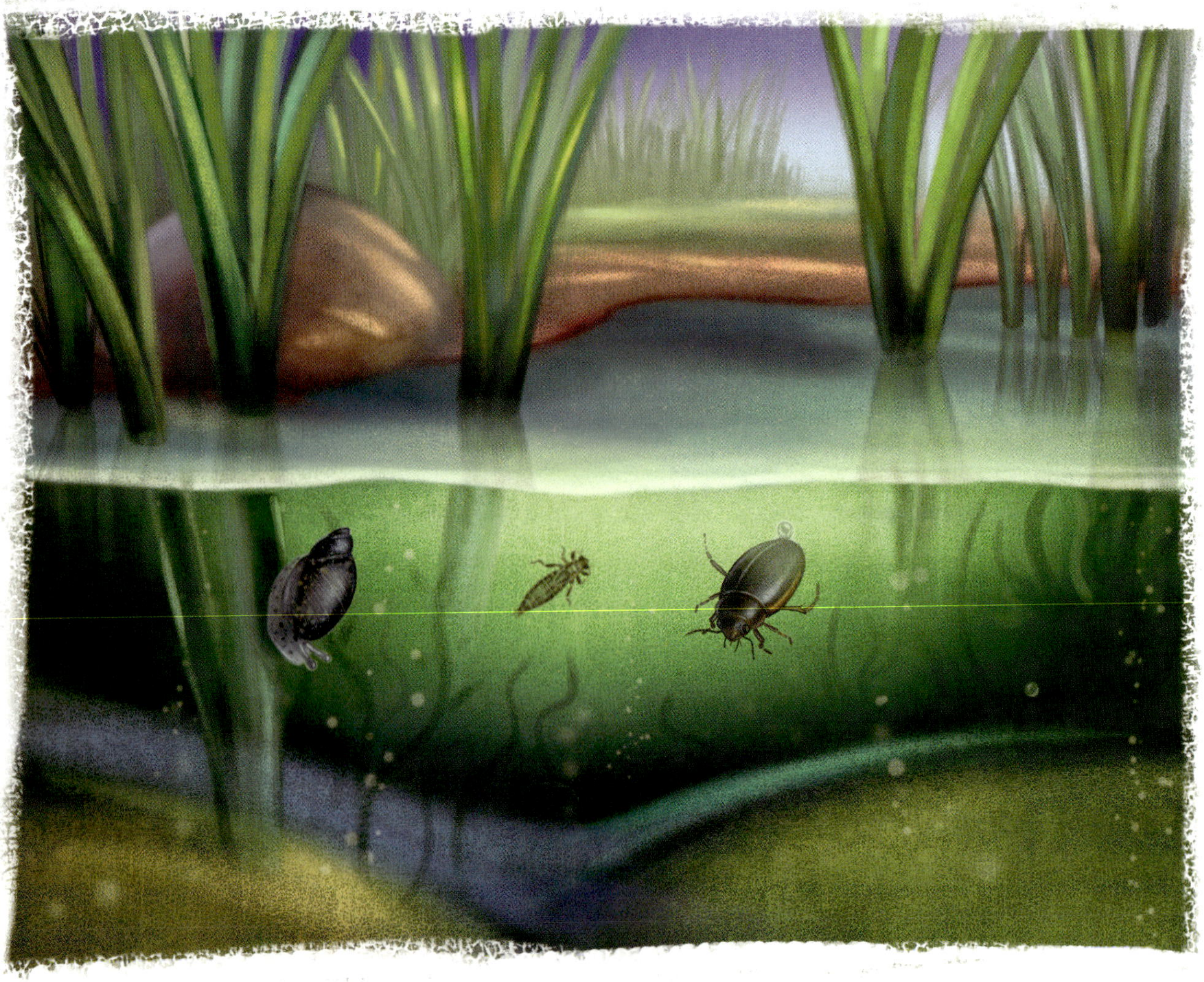

...Taddy.

NOTES FOR GOING POND PROBING

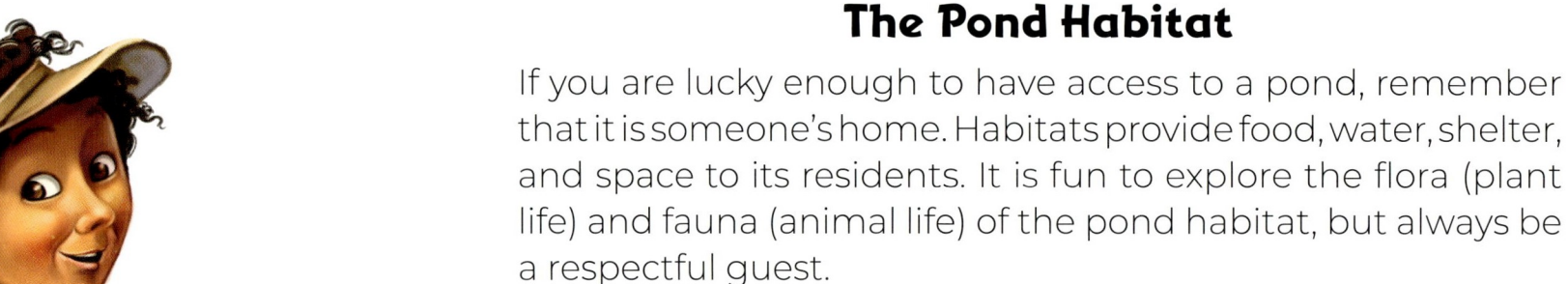

The Pond Habitat

If you are lucky enough to have access to a pond, remember that it is someone's home. Habitats provide food, water, shelter, and space to its residents. It is fun to explore the flora (plant life) and fauna (animal life) of the pond habitat, but always be a respectful guest.

The Pond Community

The pond community is made up of producers (plant life), consumers (those that eat the plants or other consumers), and decomposers (those that eat the stuff that dies). All three types of inhabitants are necessary for the community to sustain itself, as they each fill different important jobs, or niches.

Damselfly Nymph

Pond Snail

Leech

Metamorphosis in Fresh Water Habitats

Insects and many vertebrate animals undergo some kind of metamorphosis or "body/shape change" as they grow from egg to immature stage to adult stage. Frogs, toads, and butterflies are well known in this regard. But many of the critters you may catch in the pond are in the immature stage. Dragonflies, damselflies, and crane flies are all flying insects that you would recognize in the air, but look quite different in their immature stages in the water. Use a pond guide to help you know who is who in the pond. These critters have amazing adaptations to survive in the water and out.

Pond Probing

It doesn't take much to catch critters in a pond. Grab a recycled plastic cup (yogurt cups are great), a strainer or net, a plastic spoon, and a cheap paintbrush. Like Ms. Nye explains in this book, make sure to fill your cup with water before probing so that, when you catch a critter, you have a place to put it. Gently scoop the pond bottom, trying not to disturb and scoop up too much debris. Watch the water drain away and see what moves in the muck in the strainer. Use the paintbrush to pick up or coax small critters out of the strainer, since plastic spoons can be too hard on their tiny bodies. You can brush the critter on to the spoon to transfer it to the cup. Then examine and be amazed!

For General Exploration of the Outdoors:

1. Safety First: Wear sunscreen, a hat, and protective clothing for any outdoor exploration.
2. Know your poison ivy and always check the pond area before probing.
3. Be gentle with the critters you catch; handle them as little as possible.
4. Any wildlife that does not show fear is wildlife you need to get away from!
5. **Can you keep it?** You know the answer!

Dragonfly Nymph

Diving Beetle

Water Scorpion

ABOUT THE AUTHOR:

First off, Connie Nye is not related to Bill Nye the Science Guy, as much as she would like to be! Connie has worked with children in the field of science teaching, recreation, and environmental education for a very long time. She is the embodiment of her late father's mantra, "Work is fun; it's fun that's work." Connie loves her work with kids of all ages in the outdoors, especially when that work leads to a deeper understanding and respect for our natural world. Connie lives in the Brandywine Watershed (outside of Philadelphia), has two daughters, and a cat. When not in the Brandywine Watershed, Connie can be found in St. Petersburg, Florida, where her daughters and her granddog reside.

ABOUT THE ILLUSTRATOR:

Anne Wertheim has been working as a freelance illustrator for the past 20 years. During her career she has worked for numerous publishers and has illustrated many children's books and wonderful book covers. She's also very active illustrating for the advertising industry, creating great concepts for packaging and posters. Anne lives with her family on the beautiful island of Maui, in the middle of the Pacific Ocean. She has a daughter, a son, and a wonderful husband. She can often be found walking in nature with her husband and their black Labrador dog.

PRAISE FOR CAN HE KEEP IT?

"I love the concept which reminds me a tiny bit of the Salamander Room, which is a favorite of mine. I like how you told the story."

*Dr. Dawn Lawless, Principal,
Beaver Creek Elementary*

"I LOVE the idea you came up with. It will definitely make the children think before they want to keep!"

*-Ellen Eisele, Retired 1st Grade Teacher,
Barth Elementary School*

"Liked all of it; liked the real pictures of the critters; liked how it started and ended the same way."

*-Susan Zuraski and her 3rd Graders,
Beaver Creek Elementary School*

"I LOVE IT!! I think it's great. We do a trip to Rye beach with the nature center and of course get that same question! I think you did an excellent job."

*-Debbie Nye, Kindergarten Assistant Teacher,
Midland School*

"I read the book to the kids and they really liked it. I did too! Here were some comments:

'I liked the ending.' 'The book was funny.'

The consensus was all positive and you know how first grade is."

*-Noelle Messina and her 1st Graders,
Beaver Creek Elementary School*

"That was a really good book. I've done that before - I've said 'Can I keep it?' to a little tadpole before. The giant part was a good point - I can relate to it, so I wouldn't do it again."

*-Sage Connelly,
Wilmington Montessori School 1st Grader*

"The giant part was a really great way to explain why you shouldn't take things home with you because I know it would be good for your enjoyment but not theirs so you did a really good job explaining it."

*-Maya Connelly,
Wilmington Montessori School 5th Grader*

Other books by Connie Nye:

Sweet Water Hunt
An interactive watershed mystery

Pete the Shad Sings Along the Brandywine
A sing-along book of parodies to learn about watersheds

Available on Amazon,
www.sweetwatered.com
or email connie@sweetwatered.com

Most of us know that, like Tyson, we live
on a planet (Earth),
 in a country (United States),
  in a state (Pennsylvania),
   in a county (Chester).

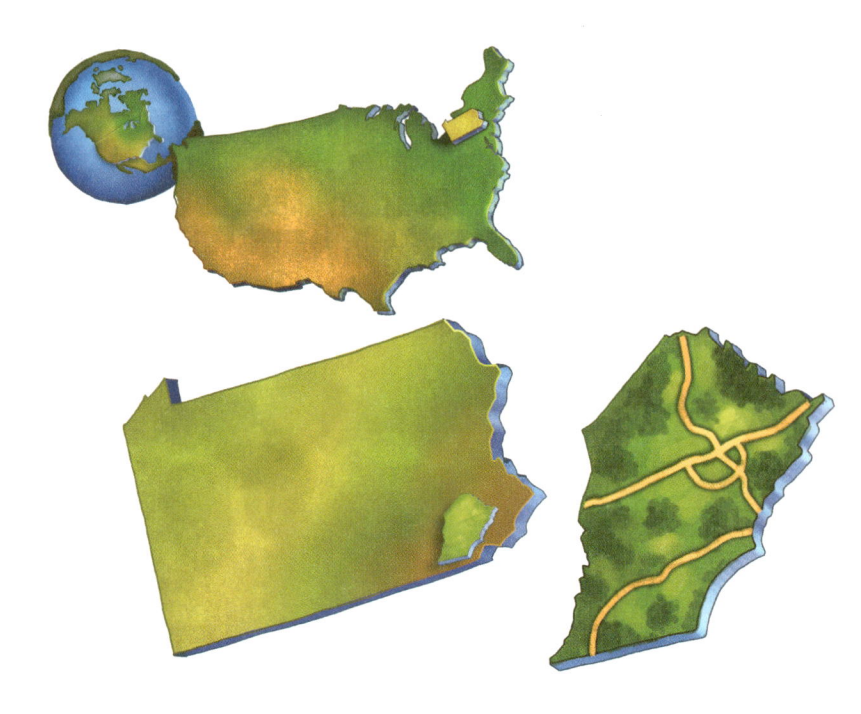

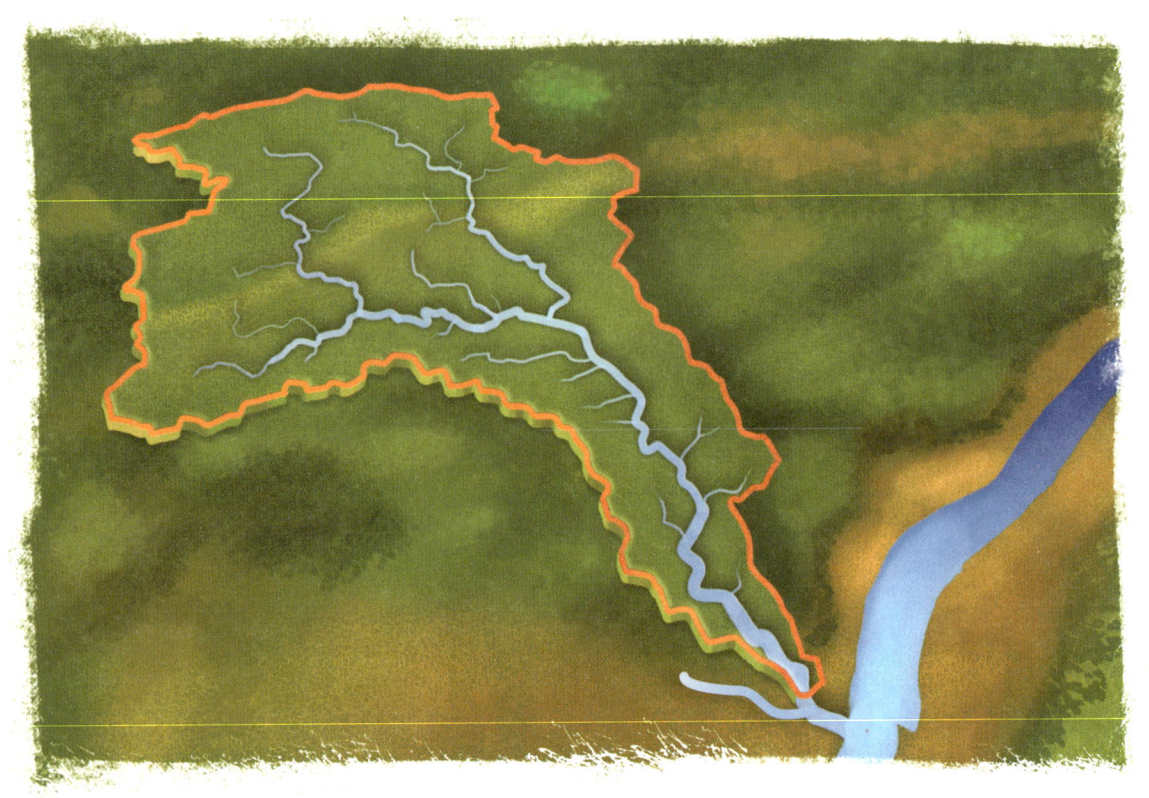

But did you know
that we also live
in a set of watersheds?
Tyson and Taddy live
in the same watersheds.